AF668141

POLITICAL IDEALS

BERTRAND RUSSELL

CLASSY
PUBLISHING

POLITICAL IDEALS
by Bertrand Russell

Published by Classy Publishing, 2023

www.classypublishing.com
info@classypublishing.com

ISBN: 978-93-5522-308-1

No part of this publication may be reproduced, stored in a retrieval system, or transmitted, in any form or by any means, electronic, mechanical, photocopying, recording or otherwise, without the prior permission of the publisher.

Typeset in Minion Pro
Cover Design by Classy Publishing

CONTENTS

CHAPTER I

Political Ideals

In dark days, men need a clear faith and a well-grounded hope; and as the outcome of these, the calm courage which takes no account of hardships by the way. The times through which we are passing have afforded to many of us a confirmation of our faith. We see that the things we had thought evil are really evil, and we know more definitely than we ever did before the directions in which men must move if a better world is to arise on the ruins of the one which is now hurling itself into destruction. We see that men's political dealings with one another are based on wholly wrong ideals, and can only be saved by quite different ideals from continuing to be a source of suffering, devastation, and sin.

Political ideals must be based upon ideals for the individual life. The aim of politics should be to make the lives of individuals as good as possible. There is nothing for the politician to consider outside or above the various men, women, and children who compose the world. The problem of politics is to adjust the relations of human beings in such a way that each severally may have as much of good in his existence as possible. And this problem requires that we should first consider what it is that we think good in the individual life.

To begin with, we do not want all men to be alike. We do not want to lay down a pattern or type to which men of all sorts are to be made by some means or another to approximate. This is the ideal of the impatient administrator. A bad teacher will aim at imposing his opinion, and turning out a set of pupils all of whom will give the same definite answer on a doubtful point. Mr. Bernard Shaw is said to hold that *Troilus and Cressida* is the best of Shakespeare's plays. Although I disagree with this opinion, I should welcome it in a pupil as a sign of individuality; but most teachers would not tolerate such a heterodox view. Not only teachers, but all commonplace persons in authority, desire in their subordinates that kind of uniformity which makes their actions easily predictable and never inconvenient. The result is that they crush initiative and individuality when they can, and when they cannot, they quarrel with it.

It is not one ideal for all men, but a separate ideal for each separate man, that has to be realized if possible. Every man has it in his being to develop into something good or bad: there is a best possible for him, and a worst possible. His circumstances will determine whether his capacities for good are developed or crushed, and whether his bad impulses are strengthened or gradually diverted into better channels.

But although we cannot set up in any detail an ideal of character which is to be universally applicable—although we cannot say, for instance, that all men ought to be industrious, or self-sacrificing, or fond of music—there are some broad principles which can be used to guide our estimates as to what is possible or desirable.

We may distinguish two sorts of goods, and two corresponding sorts of impulses. There are goods in regard to which individual possession is possible, and there are goods in which all can share alike. The food and clothing of one man is not the food and clothing of another; if the supply is insufficient, what one man has is obtained at the expense of some other man. This applies to material goods generally, and therefore to the greater part of the present economic life of the world. On the other hand, mental and spiritual goods do not belong to one man to the exclusion of another. If one man knows a science, that does not prevent others from knowing it; on the contrary, it helps them to acquire the knowledge. If one man is a great artist or poet, that does not prevent others from painting pictures or writing poems, but helps to create the atmosphere in which such things are possible. If one man is full of good-will toward others, that does not mean that there is less good-will to be shared among the rest; the more good-will one man has, the more he is likely to create among others. In such matters there is no *possession*, because there is not a definite amount to be shared; any increase anywhere tends to produce an increase everywhere.

There are two kinds of impulses, corresponding to the two kinds of goods. There are *possessive* impulses, which aim at acquiring or retaining private goods that cannot be shared; these center in the impulse of property. And there are *creative* or constructive impulses, which aim at bringing into the world or making available for use the kind of goods in which there is no privacy and no possession.

The best life is the one in which the creative impulses play the largest part and the possessive impulses the smallest. This is no new discovery. The Gospel says: "Take no thought, saying, What shall we eat? or What shall we drink? or, Wherewithal shall we be clothed?" The thought we give to these things is taken away from matters of more importance. And what is worse, the habit of mind engendered by thinking of these things is a bad one; it leads to competition, envy, domination, cruelty, and almost all the moral evils that infest the world. In particular, it leads to the predatory use of force. Material possessions can be taken by force and enjoyed by the robber. Spiritual possessions cannot be taken in this way. You may kill an artist or a thinker, but you cannot acquire his art or his thought. You may put a man to death because he loves his fellow-men, but you will not by so doing acquire the love which made his happiness. Force is impotent in such matters; it is only as regards material goods that it is effective. For this reason the men who believe in force are the men whose thoughts and desires are preoccupied with material goods.

The possessive impulses, when they are strong, infect activities which ought to be purely creative. A man who has made some valuable discovery may be filled with jealousy of a rival discoverer. If one man has found a cure for cancer and another has found a cure for consumption, one of them may be delighted if the other man's discovery turns out a mistake, instead of regretting the suffering of patients which would otherwise have been avoided. In such cases, instead of desiring knowledge for its own sake, or for the sake of its usefulness, a man is desiring it as a means to reputation. Every creative impulse is shadowed by a possessive impulse; even the aspirant to saintliness may be jealous of the more successful saint. Most affection is accompanied by some tinge of jealousy, which is a possessive impulse intruding into the creative region. Worst of all, in this direction, is the sheer envy of those who have missed everything worth having in life, and who are instinctively bent on preventing others from enjoying what they have not had. There is often much of this in the attitude of the old toward the young.

There is in human beings, as in plants and animals, a certain natural impulse of growth, and this is just as true of mental as of physical development. Physical development is helped by air and nourishment and exercise, and may be hindered by the sort of treatment which made Chinese women's feet small. In just the same way mental development may be helped or hindered by outside influences. The outside influences that help are those that merely provide encouragement or mental food or opportunities for exercising mental faculties. The influences that hinder are those that interfere with growth by applying any kind of force, whether discipline or authority or fear or the tyranny of public opinion or the necessity of engaging in some totally incongenial occupation. Worst of all influences are those that thwart or twist a man's fundamental impulse, which is what shows itself as conscience in the moral sphere; such influences are likely to do a man an inward danger from which he will never recover.

Those who realize the harm that can be done to others by any use of force against them, and the worthlessness of the goods that can be acquired by force, will be very full of respect for the liberty of others; they will not try to bind them or fetter them; they will be slow to judge and swift to sympathize; they will treat every human being with a kind of tenderness, because the principle of good in him is at once fragile and infinitely precious. They will not condemn those who are unlike themselves; they will know and feel that individuality brings differences and uniformity means death. They will wish each human being to be as much a living thing and as little a mechanical product as it is possible to be; they will cherish in each one just those things which the harsh usage of a ruthless world would destroy. In one word, all their dealings with others will be inspired by a deep impulse of *reverence*.

What we shall desire for individuals is now clear: strong creative impulses, overpowering and absorbing the instinct of possession; reverence for others; respect for the fundamental creative impulse in ourselves. A certain kind of self-respect or native pride is necessary to a good life; a man must not have a sense of utter inward defeat if he is to remain whole, but must feel the courage and the hope and the will to live by the best that is in him, whatever outward or inward obstacles it may encounter. So far as it lies in a man's own power, his life will realize its best possibilities if it has three things: creative rather than possessive impulses, reverence for others, and respect for the fundamental impulse in himself.

Political and social institutions are to be judged by the good or harm that they do to individuals. Do they encourage creativeness rather than possessiveness? Do they embody or promote a spirit of reverence between human beings? Do they preserve self-respect?

In all these ways the institutions under which we live are very far indeed from what they ought to be.

Institutions, and especially economic systems, have a profound influence in molding the characters of men and women. They may encourage adventure and hope, or timidity and the pursuit of safety. They may open men's minds to great possibilities, or close them against everything but the risk of obscure misfortune. They may make a man's happiness depend upon what he adds to the general possessions of the world, or upon what he can secure for himself of the private goods in which others cannot share. Modern capitalism forces the wrong decision of these alternatives upon all who are not heroic or exceptionally fortunate.

Men's impulses are molded, partly by their native disposition, partly by opportunity and environment, especially early environment. Direct preaching can do very little to change impulses, though it can lead people to restrain the direct expression of them, often with the result that the impulses go underground and come to the surface again in some contorted form. When we have discovered what kinds of impulse we desire, we must not rest content with preaching, or with trying to produce the outward manifestation without the inner spring; we must try rather to alter institutions in the way that will, of itself, modify the life of impulse in the desired direction.

At present our institutions rest upon two things: property and power. Both of these are very unjustly distributed; both, in the actual world, are of great importance to the happiness of the individual. Both are possessive goods; yet without them many of the goods in which all might share are hard to acquire as things are now.

Without property, as things are, a man has no freedom, and no security for the necessities of a tolerable life; without power, he has no opportunity for initiative. If men are to have free play for their creative impulses, they must be liberated from sordid cares by a certain measure of security, and they must have a sufficient share of power to be able to exercise initiative as regards the course and conditions of their lives.

Few men can succeed in being creative rather than possessive in a world which is wholly built on competition, where the great majority would fall into utter destitution if they became careless as to the acquisition of material goods, where honor and power and respect are given to wealth rather than to wisdom, where the law embodies and consecrates the injustice of those who have toward those who have not. In such an environment even those whom nature has endowed with great creative gifts become infected with the poison of competition. Men combine in groups to attain more strength in the scramble for material goods, and loyalty to the group spreads a halo of quasi-idealism round the central impulse of greed. Trade-unions and the Labor party are no more exempt from this vice than other parties and other sections of society; though they are largely inspired by the hope of a radically better world. They are too often led astray by the immediate object of securing for themselves a large share of material goods. That this desire is in accordance with justice, it is impossible to deny; but something larger and more constructive is needed as a political ideal, if the victors of to-morrow are not to become the oppressors of the day after. The inspiration and outcome of a reforming movement ought to be freedom and a generous spirit, not niggling restrictions and regulations.

The present economic system concentrates initiative in the hands of a small number of very rich men. Those who are not capitalists have, almost always, very little choice as to their activities when once they have selected a trade or profession; they are not part of the power that moves the mechanism, but only a passive portion of the machinery. Despite political democracy, there is still an extraordinary degree of difference in the power of self-direction belonging to a capitalist and to a man who has to earn his living. Economic affairs touch men's lives, at most times, much more intimately than political questions. At present the man who has no capital usually has to sell himself to some large organization, such as a railway company, for example. He has no voice in its management, and no liberty in politics except what his trade-union can secure for him. If he happens to desire a form of liberty which is not thought important by his trade-union, he is powerless; he must submit or starve.

Exactly the same thing happens to professional men. Probably a majority of journalists are engaged in writing for newspapers whose politics they disagree with; only a man of wealth can own a large newspaper, and only an accident can enable the point of view or the interests of those who are not wealthy to find expression in a newspaper. A large part of the best brains of the country are in the civil service, where the condition of their employment is silence about the evils which cannot be concealed from them. A Nonconformist minister loses his livelihood if his views displease his congregation; a member of Parliament loses his seat if he is not sufficiently supple or sufficiently stupid to follow or share all the turns and twists of public opinion. In every walk of life, independence of mind is punished by failure, more and more as economic organizations grow larger and more rigid. Is it surprising that men become increasingly docile, increasingly ready to submit to dictation and to forego the right of thinking for themselves? Yet along such lines civilization can only sink into a Byzantine immobility.

Fear of destitution is not a motive out of which a free creative life can grow, yet it is the chief motive which inspires the daily work of most wage-earners. The hope of possessing more wealth and power than any man ought to have, which is the corresponding motive of the rich, is quite as bad in its effects; it compels men to close their minds against justice, and to prevent themselves from thinking honestly on social questions while in the depths of their hearts they uneasily feel that their pleasures are bought by the miseries of others. The injustices of destitution and wealth alike ought to be rendered impossible. Then a great fear would be removed from the lives of the many, and hope would have to take on a better form in the lives of the few.

But security and liberty are only the negative conditions for good political institutions. When they have been won, we need also the positive condition: encouragement of creative energy. Security alone might produce a smug and stationary society; it demands creativeness as its counterpart, in order to keep alive the adventure and interest of life, and the movement toward perpetually new and better things. There can be no final goal for human institutions; the best are those that most encourage progress toward others still better. Without effort and change, human life cannot remain good. It is not a finished Utopia that we ought to desire, but a world where imagination and hope are alive and active.

It is a sad evidence of the weariness mankind has suffered from excessive toil that his heavens have usually been places where nothing ever happened or changed. Fatigue produces the illusion that only rest is needed for happiness; but when men have rested for a time, boredom drives them to renewed activity. For this reason, a happy life must be one in which there is activity. If it is also to be a useful life, the activity ought to be as far as possible creative, not merely predatory or defensive. But creative activity requires imagination and originality, which are apt to be subversive of the *status quo*. At present, those who have power dread a disturbance of the *status quo*, lest their unjust privileges should be taken away. In combination with the instinct for conventionality,[1] which man shares with the other gregarious animals, those who profit by the existing order have established a system which punishes originality and starves imagination from the moment of first going to school down to the time of death and burial. The whole spirit in which education is conducted needs to be changed, in order that children may be encouraged to think and feel for themselves, not to acquiesce passively in the thoughts and feelings of others. It is not rewards after the event that will produce initiative, but a certain mental atmosphere. There have been times when such an atmosphere existed: the great days of Greece, and Elizabethan England, may serve as examples. But in our own day the tyranny of vast machine-like organizations, governed from above by men who know and care little for the lives of those whom they control, is killing individuality and freedom of mind, and forcing men more and more to conform to a uniform pattern.

Vast organizations are an inevitable element in modern life, and it is useless to aim at their abolition, as has been done by

[1] In England this is called "a sense of humor."

some reformers, for instance, William Morris. It is true that they make the preservation of individuality more difficult, but what is needed is a way of combining them with the greatest possible scope for individual initiative.

One very important step toward this end would be to render democratic the government of every organization. At present, our legislative institutions are more or less democratic, except for the important fact that women are excluded. But our administration is still purely bureaucratic, and our economic organizations are monarchical or oligarchic. Every limited liability company is run by a small number of self-appointed or coöpted directors. There can be no real freedom or democracy until the men who do the work in a business also control its management.

Another measure which would do much to increase liberty would be an increase of self-government for subordinate groups, whether geographical or economic or defined by some common belief, like religious sects. A modern state is so vast and its machinery is so little understood that even when a man has a vote he does not feel himself any effective part of the force which determines its policy. Except in matters where he can act in conjunction with an exceptionally powerful group, he feels himself almost impotent, and the government remains a remote impersonal circumstance, which must be simply endured, like the weather. By a share in the control of smaller bodies, a man might regain some of that sense of personal opportunity and responsibility which belonged to the citizen of a city-state in ancient Greece or medieval Italy.

When any group of men has a strong corporate consciousness—such as belongs, for example, to a nation or a trade or a religious body—liberty demands that it should be free to decide for itself all matters which are of great importance to the outside world. This is the basis of the universal claim for national independence. But nations are by no means the only groups which ought to have self-government for their internal concerns. And nations, like other groups, ought not to have complete liberty of action in matters which are of equal concern to foreign nations. Liberty demands self-government, but not the right to interfere with others. The greatest degree of liberty is not secured by anarchy. The reconciliation of liberty with government is a difficult problem, but it is one which any political theory must face.

The essence of government is the use of force in accordance with law to secure certain ends which the holders of power consider desirable. The coercion of an individual or a group by force is always in itself more or less harmful. But if there were no government, the result would not be an absence of force in men's relations to each other; it would merely be the exercise of force by those who had strong predatory instincts, necessitating either slavery or a perpetual readiness to repel force with force on the part of those whose instincts were less violent. This is the state of affairs at present in international relations, owing to the fact that no international government exists. The results of anarchy between states should suffice to persuade us that anarchism has no solution to offer for the evils of the world.

There is probably one purpose, and only one, for which the use of force by a government is beneficent, and that is to diminish the total amount of force used m the world. It is clear, for example, that the legal prohibition of murder diminishes the total amount of violence in the world. And no one would maintain that parents should have unlimited freedom to ill-treat their children. So long as some men wish to do violence to others, there cannot be complete liberty, for either the wish to do violence must be restrained, or the victims must be left to suffer. For this reason, although individuals and societies should have the utmost freedom as regards their own affairs, they ought not to have complete freedom as regards their dealings with others. To give freedom to the strong to oppress the weak is not the way to secure the greatest possible amount of freedom in the world. This is the basis of the socialist revolt against the kind of freedom which used to be advocated by *laissez-faire* economists.

Democracy is a device—the best so far invented—for diminishing as much as possible the interference of governments with liberty. If a nation is divided into two sections which cannot both have their way, democracy theoretically insures that the majority shall have their way. But democracy is not at all an adequate device unless it is accompanied by a very great amount of devolution. Love of uniformity, or the mere pleasure of interfering, or dislike of differing tastes and temperaments, may often lead a majority to control a minority in matters which do not really concern the majority. We should none of us like to have the internal affairs of Great Britain settled by a parliament of the world, if ever such a body came into existence. Nevertheless, there are matters which such a body could settle much better than any existing instrument of government.

The theory of the legitimate use of force in human affairs, where a government exists, seems clear. Force should only be used against those who attempt to use force against others, or against those who will not respect the law in cases where a common decision is necessary and a minority are opposed to the action of the majority. These seem legitimate occasions for the use of force; and they should be legitimate occasions in international affairs, if an international government existed. The problem of the legitimate occasions for the use of force in the absence of a government is a different one, with which we are not at present concerned.

Although a government must have the power to use force, and may on occasion use it legitimately, the aim of the reformers to have such institutions as will diminish the need for actual coercion will be found to have this effect. Most of us abstain, for instance, from theft, not because it is illegal, but because we feel no desire to steal. The more men learn to live creatively rather than possessively, the less their wishes will lead them to thwart others or to attempt violent interference with their liberty. Most of the conflicts of interests, which lead individuals or organizations into disputes, are purely imaginary, and would be seen to be so if men aimed more at the goods in which all can share, and less at those private possessions that are the source of strife. In proportion as men live creatively, they cease to wish to interfere with others by force. Very many matters in which, at present, common action is thought indispensable, might well be left to individual decision. It used to be thought absolutely necessary that all the inhabitants of a country should have the same religion, but we now know that there is no such necessity. In like manner it will be found, as men grow more tolerant in their instincts, that many uniformities now insisted upon are useless and even harmful.

Good political institutions would weaken the impulse toward force and domination in two ways: first, by increasing the opportunities for the creative impulses, and by shaping education so as to strengthen these impulses; secondly, by diminishing the outlets for the possessive instincts. The diffusion of power, both in the political and the economic sphere, instead of its concentration in the hands of officials and captains of industry, would greatly diminish the opportunities for acquiring the habit of command, out of which the desire for exercising tyranny is apt to spring. Autonomy, both for districts and for organizations, would leave fewer occasions when governments were called upon to make decisions as to other people's concerns. And the abolition of capitalism and the wage system would remove the chief incentive to fear and greed, those correlative passions by which all free life is choked and gagged.

Few men seem to realize how many of the evils from which we suffer are wholly unnecessary, and that they could be abolished by a united effort within a few years. If a majority in every civilized country so desired, we could, within twenty years, abolish all abject poverty, quite half the illness in the world, the whole economic slavery which binds down nine tenths of our population; we could fill the world with beauty and joy, and secure the reign of universal peace. It is only because men are apathetic that this is not achieved, only because imagination is sluggish, and what always has been is regarded as what always must be. With good-will, generosity, intelligence, these things could be brought about.

CHAPTER II

Capitalism and the Wage System

I

The world is full of preventible evils which most men would be glad to see prevented.

Nevertheless, these evils persist, and nothing effective is done toward abolishing them.

This paradox produces astonishment in inexperienced reformers, and too often produces disillusionment in those who have come to know the difficulty of changing human institutions.

War is recognized as an evil by an immense majority in every civilized country; but this recognition does not prevent war.

The unjust distribution of wealth must be obviously an evil to those who are not prosperous, and they are nine tenths of the population. Nevertheless it continues unabated.

The tyranny of the holders of power is a source of needless suffering and misfortune to very large sections of mankind; but power remains in few hands, and tends, if anything, to grow more concentrated.

I wish first to study the evils of our present institutions, and the causes of the very limited success of reformers in the past, and then to suggest reasons for the hope of a more lasting and permanent success in the near future.

The war has come as a challenge to all who desire a better world. The system which cannot save mankind from such an appalling disaster is at fault somewhere, and cannot be amended in any lasting way unless the danger of great wars in the future can be made very small.

But war is only the final flower of an evil tree. Even in times of peace, most men live lives of monotonous labor, most women are condemned to a drudgery which almost kills the possibility of happiness before youth is past, most children are allowed to grow up in ignorance of all that would enlarge their thoughts or stimulate their imagination. The few who are more fortunate are rendered illiberal by their unjust privileges, and oppressive through fear of the awakening indignation of the masses. From the highest to the lowest, almost all men are absorbed in the economic struggle: the struggle to acquire what is their due or to retain what is not their due. Material possessions, in fact or in desire, dominate our outlook, usually to the exclusion of all generous and creative impulses. Possessiveness—the passion to have and to hold—is the ultimate source of war, and the foundation of all the ills from which the political world is suffering. Only by diminishing the strength of this passion and its hold upon our daily lives can new institutions bring permanent benefit to mankind.

Institutions which will diminish the sway of greed are possible, but only through a complete reconstruction of our whole economic system. Capitalism and the wage system must be abolished; they are twin monsters which are eating up the life of the world. In place of them we need a system which will hold in cheek men's predatory impulses, and will diminish the economic injustice that allows some to be rich in idleness while others are poor in spite of unremitting labor; but above all we need a system which will destroy the tyranny of the employer, by making men at the same time secure against destitution and able to find scope for individual initiative in the control of the industry by which they live. A better system can do all these things, and can be established by the democracy whenever it grows weary of enduring evils which there is no reason to endure.

We may distinguish four purposes at which an economic system may aim: first, it may aim at the greatest possible production of goods and at facilitating technical progress; second, it may aim at securing distributive justice; third, it may aim at giving security against destitution; and, fourth, it may aim at liberating creative impulses and diminishing possessive impulses.

Of these four purposes the last is the most important. Security is chiefly important as a means to it. State socialism, though it might give material security and more justice than we have at present, would probably fail to liberate creative impulses or produce a progressive society.

Our present system fails in all four purposes. It is chiefly defended on the ground that it achieves the first of the four purposes, namely, the greatest possible production of material goods, but it only does this in a very short-sighted way, by methods which are wasteful in the long run both of human material and of natural resources.

Capitalistic enterprise involves a ruthless belief in the importance of increasing material production to the utmost possible extent now and in the immediate future. In obedience to this belief, new portions of the earth's surface are continually brought under the sway of industrialism. Vast tracts of Africa become recruiting grounds for the labor required in the gold and diamond mines of the Rand, Rhodesia, and Kimberley; for this purpose, the population is demoralized, taxed, driven into revolt, and exposed to the contamination of European vice and disease. Healthy and vigorous races from Southern Europe are tempted to America, where sweating and slum life reduce their vitality if they do not actually cause their death. What damage is done to our own urban populations by the conditions under which they live, we all know. And what is true of the human riches of the world is no less true of the physical resources. The mines, forests, and wheat-fields of the world are all being exploited at a rate which must practically exhaust them at no distant date. On the side of material production, the world is living too fast; in a kind of delirium, almost all the energy of the world has rushed into the immediate production of something, no matter what, and no matter at what cost. And yet our present system is defended on the ground that it safeguards progress!

It cannot be said that our present economic system is any more successful in regard to the other three objects which ought to be aimed at. Among the many obvious evils of capitalism and the wage system, none are more glaring than that they encourage predatory instincts, that they allow economic injustice, and that they give great scope to the tyranny of the employer.

As to predatory instincts, we may say, broadly speaking, that in a state of nature there would be two ways of acquiring riches—one by production, the other by robbery. Under our existing system, although what is recognized as robbery is forbidden, there are nevertheless many ways of becoming rich without contributing anything to the wealth of the community. Ownership of land or capital, whether acquired or inherited, gives a legal right to a permanent income. Although most people have to produce in order to live, a privileged minority are able to live in luxury without producing anything at all. As these are the men who are not only the most fortunate but also the most respected, there is a general desire to enter their ranks, and a widespread unwillingness to face the fact that there is no justification whatever for incomes derived in this way. And apart from the passive enjoyment of rent or interest, the methods of acquiring wealth are very largely predatory. It is not, as a rule, by means of useful inventions, or of any other action which increases the general wealth of the community, that men amass fortunes; it is much more often by skill in exploiting or circumventing others. Nor is it only among the rich that our present régime promotes a narrowly acquisitive spirit. The constant risk of destitution compels most men to fill a great part of their time and thought with the economic struggle. There is a theory that this increases the total output of wealth by the community. But for reasons to which I shall return later, I believe this theory to be wholly mistaken.

Economic injustice is perhaps the most obvious evil of our present system. It would be utterly absurd to maintain that the men who inherit great wealth deserve better of the community than those who have to work for their living. I am not prepared to maintain that economic justice requires an exactly equal income for everybody. Some kinds of work require a larger income for efficiency than others do; but there is economic injustice as soon as a man has more than his share, unless it is because his efficiency in his work requires it, or as a reward for some definite service. But this point is so obvious that it needs no elaboration.

The modern growth of monopolies in the shape of trusts, cartels, federations of employers and so on has greatly increased the power of the capitalist to levy toll on the community. This tendency will not cease of itself, but only through definite action on the part of those who do not profit by the capitalist régime.

Unfortunately the distinction between the proletariat and the capitalist is not so sharp as it was in the minds of socialist theorizers. Trade-unions have funds in various securities; friendly societies are large capitalists; and many individuals eke out their wages by invested savings. All this increases the difficulty of any clear-cut radical change in our economic system. But it does not diminish the desirability of such a change.

Such a system as that suggested by the French syndicalists, in which each trade would be self-governing and completely independent, without the control of any central authority, would not secure economic justice. Some trades are in a much stronger bargaining position than others. Coal and transport, for example, could paralyze the national life, and could levy blackmail by threatening to do so. On the other hand, such people as school teachers, for example, could rouse very little terror by the threat of a strike and would be in a very weak bargaining position. Justice can never be secured by any system of unrestrained force exercised by interested parties in their own interests. For this reason the abolition of the state, which the syndicalists seem to desire, would be a measure not compatible with economic justice.

The tyranny of the employer, which at present robs the greater part of most men's lives of all liberty and all initiative, is unavoidable so long as the employer retains the right of dismissal with consequent loss of pay. This right is supposed to be essential in order that men may have an incentive to work thoroughly. But as men grow more civilized, incentives based on hope become increasingly preferable to those that are based on fear. It would be far better that men should be rewarded for working well than that they should be punished for working badly. This system is already in operation in the civil service, where a man is only dismissed for some exceptional degree of vice or virtue, such as murder or illegal abstention from it. Sufficient pay to ensure a livelihood ought to be given to every person who is willing to work, independently of the question whether the particular work at which he is skilled is wanted at the moment or not. If it is not wanted, some new trade which is wanted ought to be taught at the public expense. Why, for example, should a hansom-cab driver be allowed to suffer on account of the introduction of taxies? He has not committed any crime, and the fact that his work is no longer wanted is due to causes entirely outside his control. Instead of being allowed to starve, he ought to be given instruction in motor driving or in whatever other trade may seem most suitable. At present, owing to the fact that all industrial changes tend to cause hardships to some section of wage-earners, there is a tendency to technical conservatism on the part of labor, a dislike of innovations, new processes, and new methods. But such changes, if they are in the permanent interest of the community, ought to be carried out without allowing them to bring unmerited loss to those sections of the community whose labor is no longer wanted in the old form. The instinctive conservatism of mankind is sure to make all processes of production change more slowly than they should. It is a pity to add to this by the avoidable conservatism which is forced upon organized labor at present through the unjust workings of a change.

It will be said that men will not work well if the fear of dismissal does not spur them on. I think it is only a small percentage of whom this would be true at present. And those of whom it would be true might easily become industrious if they were given more congenial work or a wiser training. The residue who cannot be coaxed into industry by any such methods are probably to be regarded as pathological cases, requiring medical rather than penal treatment. And against this residue must be set the very much larger number who are now ruined in health or in morale by the terrible uncertainty of their livelihood and the great irregularity of their employment. To very many, security would bring a quite new possibility of physical and moral health.

The most dangerous aspect of the tyranny of the employer is the power which it gives him of interfering with men's activities outside their working hours. A man may be dismissed because the employer dislikes his religion or his politics, or chooses to think his private life immoral. He may be dismissed because he tries to produce a spirit of independence among his fellow employees. He may fail completely to find employment merely on the ground that he is better educated than most and therefore more dangerous. Such cases actually occur at present. This evil would not be remedied, but rather intensified, under state socialism, because, where the State is the only employer, there is no refuge from its prejudices such as may now accidentally arise through the differing opinions of different men. The State would be able to enforce any system of beliefs it happened to like, and it is almost certain that it would do so. Freedom of thought would be penalized, and all independence of spirit would die out.

Any rigid system would involve this evil. It is very necessary that there should be diversity and lack of complete systematization. Minorities must be able to live and develop their opinions freely. If this is not secured, the instinct of persecution and conformity will force all men into one mold and make all vital progress impossible.

For these reasons, no one ought to be allowed to suffer destitution so long as he or she is *willing* to work. And no kind of inquiry ought to be made into opinion or private life. It is only on this basis that it is possible to build up an economic system not founded upon tyranny and terror.

II

The power of the economic reformer is limited by the technical productivity of labor. So long as it was necessary to the bare subsistence of the human race that most men should work very long hours for a pittance, so long no civilization was possible except an aristocratic one; if there were to be men with sufficient leisure for any mental life, there had to be others who were sacrificed for the good of the few. But the time when such a system was necessary has passed away with the progress of machinery. It would be possible now, if we had a wise economic system, for all who have mental needs to find satisfaction for them. By a few hours a day of manual work, a man can produce as much as is necessary for his own subsistence; and if he is willing to forgo luxuries, that is all that the community has a right to demand of him. It ought to be open to all who so desire to do short hours of work for little pay, and devote their leisure to whatever pursuit happens to attract them. No doubt the great majority of those who chose this course would spend their time in mere amusement, as most of the rich do at present. But it could not be said, in such a society, that they were parasites upon the labor of others. And there would be a minority who would give their hours of nominal idleness to science or art or literature, or some other pursuit out of which fundamental progress may come. In all such matters, organization and system can only do harm. The one thing that can be done is to provide opportunity, without repining at the waste that results from most men failing to make good use of the opportunity.

But except in cases of unusual laziness or eccentric ambition, most men would elect to do a full day's work for a full day's pay. For these, who would form the immense majority, the important thing is that ordinary work should, as far as possible, afford interest and independence and scope for initiative. These things are more important than income, as soon as a certain minimum has been reached. They can be secured by gild socialism, by industrial self-government subject to state control as regards the relations of a trade to the rest of the community. So far as I know, they cannot be secured in any other way.

Guild socialism, as advocated by Mr. Orage and the "New Age," is associated with a polemic against "political" action, and in favor of direct economic action by trade-unions. It shares this with syndicalism, from which most of what is new in it is derived. But I see no reason for this attitude; political and economic action seem to me equally necessary, each in its own time and place. I think there is danger in the attempt to use the machinery of the present capitalist state for socialistic purposes. But there is need of political action to transform the machinery of the state, side by side with the transformation which we hope to see in economic institutions. In this country, neither transformation is likely to be brought about by a sudden revolution; we must expect each to come step by step, if at all, and I doubt if either could or should advance very far without the other.

The economic system we should ultimately wish to see would be one in which the state would be the sole recipient of economic rent, while private capitalistic enterprises should be replaced by self-governing combinations of those who actually do the work. It ought to be optional whether a man does a whole day's work for a whole day's pay, or half a day's work for half a day's pay, except in cases where such an arrangement would cause practical inconvenience. A man's pay should not cease through the accident of his work being no longer needed, but should continue so long as he is willing to work, a new trade being taught him at the public expense, if necessary. Unwillingness to work should be treated medically or educationally, when it could not be overcome by a change to some more congenial occupation.

The workers in a given industry should all be combined in one autonomous unit, and their work should not be subject to any outside control. The state should fix the price at which they produce, but should leave the industry self-governing in all other respects. In fixing prices, the state should, as far as possible, allow each industry to profit by any improvements which it might introduce into its own processes, but should endeavor to prevent undeserved loss or gain through changes in external economic conditions. In this way there would be every incentive to progress, with the least possible danger of unmerited destitution. And although large economic organizations will continue, as they are bound to do, there will be a diffusion of power which will take away the sense of individual impotence from which men and women suffer at present.

III

Some men, though they may admit that such a system would be desirable, will argue that it is impossible to bring it about, and that therefore we must concentrate on more immediate objects.

I think it must be conceded that a political party ought to have proximate aims, measures which it hopes to carry in the next session or the next parliament, as well as a more distant goal. Marxian socialism, as it existed in Germany, seemed to me to suffer in this way: although the party was numerically powerful, it was politically weak, because it had no minor measures to demand while waiting for the revolution. And when, at last, German socialism was captured by those who desired a less impracticable policy, the modification which occurred was of exactly the wrong kind: acquiescence in bad policies, such as militarism and imperialism, rather than advocacy of partial reforms which, however inadequate, would still have been steps in the right direction.

A similar defect was inherent in the policy of French syndicalism as it existed before the war. Everything was to wait for the general strike; after adequate preparation, one day the whole proletariat would unanimously refuse to work, the property owners would acknowledge their defeat, and agree to abandon all their privileges rather than starve. This is a dramatic conception; but love of drama is a great enemy of true vision. Men cannot be trained, except under very rare circumstances, to do something suddenly which is very different from what they have been doing before. If the general strike were to succeed, the victors, despite their anarchism, would be compelled at once to form an administration, to create a new police force to prevent looting and wanton destruction, to establish a provisional government issuing dictatorial orders to the various sections of revolutionaries. Now the syndicalists are opposed in principle to all political action; they would feel that they were departing from their theory in taking the necessary practical steps, and they would be without the required training because of their previous abstention from politics. For these reasons it is likely that, even after a syndicalist revolution, actual power would fall into the hands of men who were not really syndicalists.

Another objection to a program which is to be realized suddenly at some remote date by a revolution or a general strike is that enthusiasm flags when there is nothing to do meanwhile, and no partial success to lessen the weariness of waiting. The only sort of movement which can succeed by such methods is one where the sentiment and the program are both very simple, as is the case in rebellions of oppressed nations. But the line of demarcation between capitalist and wage-earner is not sharp, like the line between Turk and Armenian, or between an Englishman and a native of India. Those who have advocated the social revolution have been mistaken in their political methods, chiefly because they have not realized how many people there are in the community whose sympathies and interests lie half on the side of capital, half on the side of labor. These people make a clear-cut revolutionary policy very difficult.

For these reasons, those who aim at an economic reconstruction which is not likely to be completed to-morrow must, if they are to have any hope of success, be able to approach their goal by degrees, through measures which are of some use in themselves, even if they should not ultimately lead to the desired end. There must be activities which train men for those that they are ultimately to carry out, and there must be possible achievements in the near future, not only a vague hope of a distant paradise.

But although I believe that all this is true, I believe no less firmly that really vital and radical reform requires some vision beyond the immediate future, some realization of what human beings might make of human life if they chose. Without some such hope, men will not have the energy and enthusiasm necessary to overcome opposition, or the steadfastness to persist when their aims are for the moment unpopular. Every man who has really sincere desire for any great amelioration in the conditions of life has first to face ridicule, then persecution, then cajolery and attempts at subtle corruption. We know from painful experience how few pass unscathed through these three ordeals. The last especially, when the reformer is shown all the kingdoms of the earth, is difficult, indeed almost impossible, except for those who have made their ultimate goal vivid to themselves by clear and definite thought.

Economic systems are concerned essentially with the production and distribution of material goods. Our present system is wasteful on the production side, and unjust on the side of distribution. It involves a life of slavery to economic forces for the great majority of the community, and for the minority a degree of power over the lives of others which no man ought to have. In a good community the production of the necessaries of existence would be a mere preliminary to the important and interesting part of life, except for those who find a pleasure in some part of the work of producing necessaries. It is not in the least necessary that economic needs should dominate man as they do at present. This is rendered necessary at present, partly by the inequalities of wealth, partly by the fact that things of real value, such as a good education, are difficult to acquire, except for the well-to-do.

Private ownership of land and capital is not defensible on grounds of justice, or on the ground that it is an economical way of producing what the community needs. But the chief objections to it are that it stunts the lives of men and women, that it enshrines a ruthless possessiveness in all the respect which is given to success, that it leads men to fill the greater part of their time and thought with the acquisition of purely material goods, and that it affords a terrible obstacle to the advancement of civilization and creative energy.

The approach to a system free from these evils need not be sudden; it is perfectly possible to proceed step by step towards economic freedom and industrial self-government. It is not true that there is any outward difficulty in creating the kind of institutions that we have been considering. If organized labor wishes to create them, nothing could stand in its way. The difficulty involved is merely the difficulty of inspiring men with hope, of giving them enough imagination to see that the evils from which they suffer are unnecessary, and enough thought to understand how the evils are to be cured. This is a difficulty which can be overcome by time and energy. But it will not be overcome if the leaders of organized labor have no breadth of outlook, no vision, no hopes beyond some slight superficial improvement within the framework of the existing system. Revolutionary action may be unnecessary, but revolutionary thought is indispensable, and, as the outcome of thought, a rational and constructive hope.

CHAPTER III

Pitfalls in Socialism

I

In its early days, socialism was a revolutionary movement of which the object was the liberation of the wage-earning classes and the establishment of freedom and justice. The passage from capitalism to the new régime was to be sudden and violent: capitalists were to be expropriated without compensation, and their power was not to be replaced by any new authority.

Gradually a change came over the spirit of socialism. In France, socialists became members of the government, and made and unmade parliamentary majorities. In Germany, social democracy grew so strong that it became impossible for it to resist the temptation to barter away some of its intransigeance in return for government recognition of its claims. In England, the Fabians taught the advantage of reform as against revolution, and of conciliatory bargaining as against irreconcilable antagonism.

The method of gradual reform has many merits as compared to the method of revolution, and I have no wish to preach revolution. But gradual reform has certain dangers, to wit, the ownership or control of businesses hitherto in private hands, and by encouraging legislative interference for the benefit of various sections of the wage-earning classes. I think it is at least doubtful whether such measures do anything at all to contribute toward the ideals which inspired the early socialists and still inspire the great majority of those who advocate some form of socialism.

Let us take as an illustration such a measure as state purchase of railways. This is a typical object of state socialism, thoroughly practicable, already achieved in many countries, and clearly the sort of step that must be taken in any piecemeal approach to complete collectivism. Yet I see no reason to believe that any real advance toward democracy, freedom, or economic justice is achieved when a state takes over the railways after full compensation to the shareholders.

Economic justice demands a diminution, if not a total abolition, of the proportion of the national income which goes to the recipients of rent and interest. But when the holders of railway shares are given government stock to replace their shares, they are given the prospect of an income in perpetuity equal to what they might reasonably expect to have derived from their shares. Unless there is reason to expect a great increase in the earnings of railways, the whole operation does nothing to alter the distribution of wealth. This could only be effected if the present owners were expropriated, or paid less than the market value, or given a mere life-interest as compensation. When full value is given, economic justice is not advanced in any degree.

There is equally little advance toward freedom. The men employed on the railway have no more voice than they had before in the management of the railway, or in the wages and conditions of work. Instead of having to fight the directors, with the possibility of an appeal to the government, they now have to fight the government directly; and experience does not lead to the view that a government department has any special tenderness toward the claims of labor. If they strike, they have to contend against the whole organized power of the state, which they can only do successfully if they happen to have a strong public opinion on their side. In view of the influence which the state can always exercise on the press, public opinion is likely to be biased against them, particularly when a nominally progressive government is in power. There will no longer be the possibility of divergences between the policies of different railways. Railway men in England derived advantages for many years from the comparatively liberal policy of the North Eastern Railway, which they were able to use as an argument for a similar policy elsewhere. Such possibilities are excluded by the dead uniformity of state administration.

And there is no real advance toward democracy. The administration of the railways will be in the hands of officials whose bias and associations separate them from labor, and who will develop an autocratic temper through the habit of power. The democratic machinery by which these officials are nominally controlled is cumbrous and remote, and can only be brought into operation on first-class issues which rouse the interest of the whole nation. Even then it is very likely that the superior education of the officials and the government, combined with the advantages of their position, will enable them to mislead the public as to the issues, and alienate the general sympathy even from the most excellent cause.

I do not deny that these evils exist at present; I say only that they will not be remedied by such measures as the nationalization of railways in the present economic and political environment. A greater upheaval, and a greater change in men's habits of mind, is necessary for any really vital progress.

II

State socialism, even in a nation which possesses the form of political democracy, is not a truly democratic system. The way in which it fails to be democratic may be made plain by an analogy from the political sphere. Every democrat recognizes that the Irish ought to have self-government for Irish affairs, and ought not to be told that they have no grievance because they share in the Parliament of the United Kingdom. It is essential to democracy that any group of citizens whose interests or desires separate them at all widely from the rest of the community should be free to decide their internal affairs for themselves. And what is true of national or local groups is equally true of economic groups, such as miners or railway men. The national machinery of general elections is by no means sufficient to secure for groups of this kind the freedom which they ought to have.

The power of officials, which is a great and growing danger in the modern state, arises from the fact that the majority of the voters, who constitute the only ultimate popular control over officials, are as a rule not interested in any one particular question, and are therefore not likely to interfere effectively against an official who is thwarting the wishes of the minority who are interested. The official is nominally subject to indirect popular control, but not to the control of those who are directly affected by his action. The bulk of the public will either never hear about the matter in dispute, or, if they do hear, will form a hasty opinion based upon inadequate information, which is far more likely to come from the side of the officials than from the section of the community which is affected by the question at issue. In an important political issue, some degree of knowledge is likely to be diffused in time; but in other matters there is little hope that this will happen.

It may be said that the power of officials is much less dangerous than the power of capitalists, because officials have no economic interests that are opposed to those of wage-earners. But this argument involves far too simple a theory of political human nature—a theory which orthodox socialism adopted from the classical political economy, and has tended to retain in spite of growing evidence of its falsity. Economic self-interest, and even economic class-interest, is by no means the only important political motive. Officials, whose salary is generally quite unaffected by their decisions on particular questions, are likely, if they are of average honesty, to decide according to their view of the public interest; but their view will none the less have a bias which will often lead them wrong. It is important to understand this bias before entrusting our destinies too unreservedly to government departments.

The first thing to observe is that, in any very large organization, and above all in a great state, officials and legislators are usually very remote from those whom they govern, and not imaginatively acquainted with the conditions of life to which their decisions will be applied. This makes them ignorant of much that they ought to know, even when they are industrious and willing to learn whatever can be taught by statistics and blue-books. The one thing they understand intimately is the office routine and the administrative rules. The result is an undue anxiety to secure a uniform system. I have heard of a French minister of education taking out his watch, and remarking, "At this moment all the children of such and such an age in France are learning so and so." This is the ideal of the administrator, an ideal utterly fatal to free growth, initiative, experiment, or any far reaching innovation. Laziness is not one of the motives recognized in textbooks on political theory, because all ordinary knowledge of human nature is considered unworthy of the dignity of these works; yet we all know that laziness is an immensely powerful motive with all but a small minority of mankind.

Unfortunately, in this case laziness is reinforced by love of power, which leads energetic officials to create the systems which lazy officials like to administer. The energetic official inevitably dislikes anything that he does not control. His official sanction must be obtained before anything can be done. Whatever he finds in existence he wishes to alter in some way, so as to have the satisfaction of feeling his power and making it felt. If he is conscientious, he will think out some perfectly uniform and rigid scheme which he believes to be the best possible, and he will then impose this scheme ruthlessly, whatever promising growths he may have to lop down for the sake of symmetry. The result inevitably has something of the deadly dullness of a new rectangular town, as compared with the beauty and richness of an ancient city which has lived and grown with the separate lives and individualities of many generations. What has grown is always more living than what has been decreed; but the energetic official will always prefer the tidiness of what he has decreed to the apparent disorder of spontaneous growth.

The mere possession of power tends to produce a love of power, which is a very dangerous motive, because the only sure proof of power consists in preventing others from doing what they wish to do. The essential theory of democracy is the diffusion of power among the whole people, so that the evils produced by one man's possession of great power shall be obviated. But the diffusion of power through democracy is only effective when the voters take an interest in the question involved. When the question does not interest them, they do not attempt to control the administration, and all actual power passes into the hands of officials.

For this reason, the true ends of democracy are not achieved by state socialism or by any system which places great power in the hands of men subject to no popular control except that which is more or less indirectly exercised through parliament.

Any fresh survey of men's political actions shows that, in those who have enough energy to be politically effective, love of power is a stronger motive than economic self-interest. Love of power actuates the great millionaires, who have far more money than they can spend, but continue to amass wealth merely in order to control more and more of the world's finance.[2] Love of power is obviously the ruling motive of many politicians. It is also the chief cause of wars, which are admittedly almost always a bad speculation from the mere point of view of wealth. For this reason, a new economic system which merely attacks economic motives and does not interfere with the concentration of power is not likely to effect any very great improvement in the world. This is one of the chief reasons for regarding state socialism with suspicion.

III

The problem of the distribution of power is a more difficult one than the problem of the distribution of wealth. The machinery of representative government has concentrated on *ultimate* power as the only important matter, and has ignored immediate executive power. Almost nothing has been done to democratize administration. Government officials, in virtue of their income, security, and social position, are likely to be on the side of the rich, who have been their daily associates ever since the time of school and college. And whether or not they are on the side of the rich, they are not likely, for the reasons we have been

[2] Cf. J. A. Hobson, "The Evolution of Modern Capitalism."

considering, to be genuinely in favor of progress. What applies to government officials applies also to members of Parliament, with the sole difference that they have had to recommend themselves to a constituency. This, however, only adds hypocrisy to the other qualities of a ruling caste. Whoever has stood in the lobby of the House of Commons watching members emerge with wandering eye and hypothetical smile, until the constituent is espied, his arm taken, "my dear fellow" whispered in his ear, and his steps guided toward the inner precincts—whoever, observing this, has realized that these are the arts by which men become and remain legislators, can hardly fail to feel that democracy as it exists is not an absolutely perfect instrument of government. It is a painful fact that the ordinary voter, at any rate in England, is quite blind to insincerity. The man who does not care about any definite political measures can generally be won by corruption or flattery, open or concealed; the man who is set on securing reforms will generally prefer an ambitious windbag to a man who desires the public good without possessing a ready tongue. And the ambitious windbag, as soon as he has become a power by the enthusiasm he has aroused, will sell his influence to the governing clique, sometimes openly, sometimes by the more subtle method of intentionally failing at a crisis. This is part of the normal working of democracy as embodied in representative institutions. Yet a cure must be found if democracy is not to remain a farce.

One of the sources of evil in modern large democracies is the fact that most of the electorate have no direct or vital interest in most of the questions that arise. Should Welsh children be allowed the use of the Welsh language in schools? Should gipsies be compelled to abandon their nomadic life at the bidding of the education authorities? Should miners have an eight-hour day? Should Christian Scientists be compelled to call in doctors in case of serious illness? These are matters of passionate interest to certain sections of the community, but of very little interest to the great majority. If they are decided according to the wishes of the numerical majority, the intense desires of a minority will be overborne by the very slight and uninformed whims of the indifferent remainder. If the minority are geographically concentrated, so that they can decide elections in a certain number of constituencies, like the Welsh and the miners, they have a good chance of getting their way, by the wholly beneficent process which its enemies describe as log-rolling. But if they are scattered and politically feeble, like the gipsies and the Christian Scientists, they stand a very poor chance against the prejudices of the majority. Even when they are geographically concentrated, like the Irish, they may fail to obtain their wishes, because they arouse some hostility or some instinct of domination in the majority. Such a state of affairs is the negation of all democratic principles.

The tyranny of the majority is a very real danger. It is a mistake to suppose that the majority is necessarily right. On every new question the majority is always wrong at first. In matters where the state must act as a whole, such as tariffs, for example, decision by majorities is probably the best method that can be devised. But there are a great many questions in which there is no need of a uniform decision. Religion is recognized as one of these. Education ought to be one, provided a certain minimum standard is attained. Military service clearly ought to be one. Wherever divergent action by different groups is possible without anarchy, it ought to be permitted. In such cases it will be found by those who consider past history that, whenever any new fundamental issue arises, the majority are in the wrong, because they are guided by prejudice and habit. Progress comes through the gradual effect of a minority in converting opinion and altering custom. At one time—not so very long ago—it was considered monstrous wickedness to maintain that old women ought not to be burnt as witches. If those who held this opinion had been forcibly suppressed, we should still be steeped in medieval superstition. For such reasons, it is of the utmost importance that the majority should refrain from imposing its will as regards matters in which uniformity is not absolutely necessary.

IV

The cure for the evils and dangers which we have been considering is a very great extension of devolution and federal government. Wherever there is a national consciousness, as in Wales and Ireland, the area in which it exists ought to be allowed to decide all purely local affairs without external interference. But there are many matters which ought to be left to the management, not of local groups, but of trade groups, or of organizations embodying some set of opinions. In the East, men are subject to different laws according to the religion they profess. Something of this kind is necessary if any semblance of liberty is to exist where there is great divergence in beliefs.

Some matters are essentially geographical; for instance, gas and water, roads, tariffs, armies and navies. These must be decided by an authority representing an area. How large the area ought to be, depends upon accidents of topography and sentiment, and also upon the nature of the matter involved. Gas and water require a small area, roads a somewhat larger one, while the only satisfactory area for an army or a navy is the whole planet, since no smaller area will prevent war.

But the proper unit in most economic questions, and also in most questions that are intimately concerned with personal opinions, is not geographical at all. The internal management of railways ought not to be in the hands of the geographical state, for reasons which we have already considered. Still less ought it to be in the hands of a set of irresponsible capitalists. The only truly democratic system would be one which left the internal management of railways in the hands of the men who work on them. These men should elect the general manager, and a parliament of directors if necessary. All questions of wages, conditions of labor, running of trains, and acquisition of material, should be in the hands of a body responsible only to those actually engaged in the work of the railway.

The same arguments apply to other large trades: mining, iron and steel, cotton, and so on. British trade-unionism, it seems to me, has erred in conceiving labor and capital as both permanent forces, which were to be brought to some equality of strength by the organization of labor. This seems to me too modest an ideal. The ideal which I should wish to substitute involves the conquest of democracy and self-government in the economic sphere as in the political sphere, and the total abolition of the power now wielded by the capitalist. The man who works on a railway ought to have a voice in the government of the railway, just as much as the man who works in a state has a right to a voice in the management of his state. The concentration of business initiative in the hands of the employers is a great evil, and robs the employees of their legitimate share of interest in the larger problems of their trade.

French syndicalists were the first to advocate the system of trade autonomy as a better solution than state socialism. But in their view the trades were to be independent, almost like sovereign states at present. Such a system would not promote peace, any more than it does at present in international relations. In the affairs of any body of men, we may broadly distinguish what may be called questions of home politics from questions of foreign politics. Every group sufficiently well-marked to constitute a political entity ought to be autonomous in regard to internal matters, but not in regard to those that directly affect the outside world. If two groups are both entirely free as regards their relations to each other, there is no way of averting the danger of an open or covert appeal to force. The relations of a group of men to the outside world ought, whenever possible, to be controlled by a neutral authority. It is here that the state is necessary for adjusting the relations between different trades. The men who make some commodity should be entirely free as regards hours of labor, distribution of the total earnings of the trade, and all questions of business management. But they should not be free as regards the price of what they produce, since price is a matter concerning their relations to the rest of the community. If there were nominal freedom in regard to price, there would be a danger of a constant tug-of-war, in which those trades which were most immediately necessary to the existence of the community could always obtain an unfair advantage. Force is no more admirable in the economic sphere than in dealings between states. In order to secure the maximum of freedom with the minimum of force, the universal principle is: *Autonomy within each politically important group, and a neutral authority for deciding questions involving relations between groups.* The neutral authority should, of course, rest on a democratic basis, but should, if possible, represent a constituency wider than that of the groups concerned. In international affairs the only adequate authority would be one representing all civilized nations.

In order to prevent undue extension of the power of such authorities, it is desirable and necessary that the various autonomous groups should be very jealous of their liberties, and very ready to resist by political means any encroachments upon their independence. State socialism does not tolerate such groups, each with their own officials responsible to the group. Consequently it abandons the internal affairs of a group to the control of men not responsible to that group or specially aware of its needs. This opens the door to tyranny and to the destruction of initiative. These dangers are avoided by a system which allows any group of men to combine for any given purpose, provided it is not predatory, and to claim from the central authority such self-government as is necessary to the carrying out of the purpose. Churches of various denominations afford an instance. Their autonomy was won by centuries of warfare and persecution. It is to be hoped that a less terrible struggle will be required to achieve the same result in the economic sphere. But whatever the obstacles, I believe the importance of liberty is as great in the one case as it has been admitted to be in the other.

CHAPTER IV

Individual Liberty and Public Control

I

Society cannot exist without law and order, and cannot advance except through the initiative of vigorous innovators. Yet law and order are always hostile to innovations, and innovators are almost always, to some extent, anarchists. Those whose minds are dominated by fear of a relapse towards barbarism will emphasize the importance of law and order, while those who are inspired by the hope of an advance towards civilization will usually be more conscious of the need of individual initiative. Both temperaments are necessary, and wisdom lies in allowing each to operate freely where it is beneficent. But those who are on the side of law and order, since they are reinforced by custom and the instinct for upholding the *status quo*, have no need of a reasoned defense. It is the innovators who have difficulty in being allowed to exist and work. Each generation believes that this difficulty is a thing of the past, but each generation is only tolerant of *past* innovations. Those of its own day are met with the same persecution as though the principle of toleration had never been heard of.

"In early society," says Westermarck, "customs are not only moral rules, but the only moral rules ever thought of. The savage strictly complies with the Hegelian command that no man must have a private conscience. The following statement, which refers to the Tinnevelly Shanars, may be quoted as a typical example: 'Solitary individuals amongst them rarely adopt any new opinions, or any new course of procedure. They follow the multitude to do evil, and they follow the multitude to do good. They think in herds.'"[3]

Those among ourselves who have never thought a thought or done a deed in the slightest degree different from the thoughts and deeds of our neighbors will congratulate themselves on the difference between us and the savage. But those who have ever attempted any real innovation cannot help feeling that the people they know are not so very unlike the Tinnevelly Shanars.

Under the influence of socialism, even progressive opinion, in recent years, has been hostile to individual liberty. Liberty is associated, in the minds of reformers, with *laissez-faire*, the Manchester School, and the exploitation of women and children which resulted from what was euphemistically called "free competition." All these things were evil, and required state interference; in fact, there is need of an immense increase of state action in regard to cognate evils which still exist. In everything that concerns the economic life of the community, as regards both distribution and conditions of production, what is required is more public control, not less—how much more, I do not profess to know.

Another direction in which there is urgent need of the substitution of law and order for anarchy is international relations. At present, each sovereign state has complete individual freedom, subject only to the sanction of war. This individual freedom will have to be curtailed in regard to external relations if wars are ever to cease.

---

[3] "The Origin and Development of the Moral Ideas," 2d edition, Vol. I, p. 119.

But when we pass outside the sphere of material possessions, we find that the arguments in favor of public control almost entirely disappear.

Religion, to begin with, is recognized as a matter in which the state ought not to interfere. Whether a man is Christian, Mahometan, or Jew is a question of no public concern, so long as he obeys the laws; and the laws ought to be such as men of all religions can obey. Yet even here there are limits. No civilized state would tolerate a religion demanding human sacrifice. The English in India put an end to suttee, in spite of a fixed principle of non-interference with native religious customs. Perhaps they were wrong to prevent suttee, yet almost every European would have done the same. We cannot *effectively* doubt that such practices ought to be stopped, however we may theorize in favor of religious liberty.

In such cases, the interference with liberty is imposed from without by a higher civilization. But the more common case, and the more interesting, is when an independent state interferes on behalf of custom against individuals who are feeling their way toward more civilized beliefs and institutions.

"In New South Wales," says Westermarck, "the first-born of every lubra used to be eaten by the tribe 'as part of a religious ceremony.' In the realm of Khai-muh, in China, according to a native account, it was customary to kill and devour the eldest son alive. Among certain tribes in British Columbia the first child is often sacrificed to the sun. The Indians of Florida, according to Le Moyne de Morgues, sacrificed the first-born son to the chief...."[4]

There are pages and pages of such instances.

There is nothing analogous to these practices among ourselves. When the first-born in Florida was told that his king

[4] *Op cit.*, p. 459.

and country needed him, this was a mere mistake, and with us mistakes of this kind do not occur. But it is interesting to inquire how these superstitions died out, in such cases, for example, as that of Khai-muh, where foreign compulsion is improbable. We may surmise that some parents, under the selfish influence of parental affection, were led to doubt whether the sun would really be angry if the eldest child were allowed to live. Such rationalism would be regarded as very dangerous, since it was calculated to damage the harvest. For generations the opinion would be cherished in secret by a handful of cranks, who would not be able to act upon it. At last, by concealment or flight, a few parents would save their children from the sacrifice. Such parents would be regarded as lacking all public spirit, and as willing to endanger the community for their private pleasure. But gradually it would appear that the state remained intact, and the crops were no worse than in former years. Then, by a fiction, a child would be deemed to have been sacrificed if it was solemnly dedicated to agriculture or some other work of national importance chosen by the chief. It would be many generations before the child would be allowed to choose its own occupation after it had grown old enough to know its own tastes and capacities. And during all those generations, children would be reminded that only an act of grace had allowed them to live at all, and would exist under the shadow of a purely imaginary duty to the state.

The position of those parents who first disbelieved in the utility of infant sacrifice illustrates all the difficulties which arise in connection with the adjustment of individual freedom to public control. The authorities, believing the sacrifice necessary for the good of the community, were bound to insist upon it; the parents, believing it useless, were equally bound to do everything in their power toward saving the child. How ought both parties to act in such a case?

The duty of the skeptical parent is plain: to save the child by any possible means, to preach the uselessness of the sacrifice in season and out of season, and to endure patiently whatever penalty the law may indict for evasion. But the duty of the authorities is far less clear. So long as they remain firmly persuaded that the universal sacrifice of the first-born is indispensable, they are bound to persecute those who seek to undermine this belief. But they will, if they are conscientious, very carefully examine the arguments of opponents, and be willing in advance to admit that these arguments *may* be sound. They will carefully search their own hearts to see whether hatred of children or pleasure in cruelty has anything to do with their belief. They will remember that in the past history of Khai-muh there are innumerable instances of beliefs, now known to be false, on account of which those who disagreed with the prevalent view were put to death. Finally they will reflect that, though errors which are traditional are often wide-spread, new beliefs seldom win acceptance unless they are nearer to the truth than what they replace; and they will conclude that a new belief is probably either an advance, or so unlikely to become common as to be innocuous. All these considerations will make them hesitate before they resort to punishment.

II

The study of past times and uncivilized races makes it clear beyond question that the customary beliefs of tribes or nations are almost invariably false. It is difficult to divest ourselves completely of the customary beliefs of our own age and nation, but it is not very difficult to achieve a certain degree of doubt in regard to them. The Inquisitor who burnt men at the stake was acting with true humanity if all his beliefs were correct; but if they were in error at any point, he was inflicting a wholly unnecessary cruelty. A good working maxim in such matters is this: Do not trust customary beliefs so far as to perform actions which must be disastrous unless the beliefs in question are wholly true. The world would be utterly bad, in the opinion of the average Englishman, unless he could say "Britannia rules the waves"; in the opinion of the average German, unless he could say "Deutschland über alles." For the sake of these beliefs, they are willing to destroy European civilization. If the beliefs should happen to be false, their action is regrettable.

One fact which emerges from these considerations is that no obstacle should be placed in the way of thought and its expression, nor yet in the way of statements of fact. This was formerly common ground among liberal thinkers, though it was never quite realized in the practice of civilized countries. But it has recently become, throughout Europe, a dangerous paradox, on account of which men suffer imprisonment or starvation. For this reason it has again become worth stating. The grounds for it are so evident that I should be ashamed to repeat them if they were not universally ignored. But in the actual world it is very necessary to repeat them.

To attain complete truth is not given to mortals, but to advance toward it by successive steps is not impossible. On any matter of general interest, there is usually, in any given community at any given time, a received opinion, which is accepted as a matter of course by all who give no special thought to the matter. Any questioning of the received opinion rouses hostility, for a number of reasons.

The most important of these is the instinct of conventionality, which exists in all gregarious animals and often leads them to put to death any markedly peculiar member of the herd.

The next most important is the feeling of insecurity aroused by doubt as to the beliefs by which we are in the habit of regulating our lives. Whoever has tried to explain the philosophy of Berkeley to a plain man will have seen in its unadulterated form the anger aroused by this feeling. What the plain man derives from Berkeley's philosophy at a first hearing is an uncomfortable suspicion that nothing is solid, so that it is rash to sit on a chair or to expect the floor to sustain us. Because this suspicion is uncomfortable, it is irritating, except to those who regard the whole argument as merely nonsense. And in a more or less analogous way any questioning of what has been taken for granted destroys the feeling of standing on solid ground, and produces a condition of bewildered fear.

A third reason which makes men dislike novel opinions is that vested interests are bound up with old beliefs. The long fight of the church against science, from Giordano Bruno to Darwin, is attributable to this motive among others. The horror of socialism which existed in the remote past was entirely attributable to this cause. But it would be a mistake to assume, as is done by those who seek economic motives everywhere, that vested interests are the principal source of anger against novelties in thought. If this were the case, intellectual progress would be much more rapid than it is.

The instinct of conventionality, horror of uncertainty, and vested interests, all militate against the acceptance of a new idea. And it is even harder to think of a new idea than to get it accepted; most people might spend a lifetime in reflection without ever making a genuinely original discovery.

In view of all these obstacles, it is not likely that any society at any time will suffer from a plethora of heretical opinions. Least of all is this likely in a modern civilized society, where the conditions of life are in constant rapid change, and demand, for successful adaptation, an equally rapid change in intellectual outlook. There should be an attempt, therefore, to encourage, rather than discourage, the expression of new beliefs and the dissemination of knowledge tending to support them. But the very opposite is, in fact, the case. From childhood upward, everything is done to make the minds of men and women conventional and sterile. And if, by misadventure, some spark of imagination remains, its unfortunate possessor is considered unsound and dangerous, worthy only of contempt in time of peace and of prison or a traitor's death in time of war. Yet such men are known to have been in the past the chief benefactors of mankind, and are the very men who receive most honor as soon as they are safely dead.

The whole realm of thought and opinion is utterly unsuited to public control; it ought to be as free, and as spontaneous as is possible to those who know what others have believed. The state is justified in insisting that children shall be educated, but it is not justified in forcing their education to proceed on a uniform plan and to be directed to the production of a dead level of glib uniformity. Education, and the life of the mind generally, is a matter in which individual initiative is the chief thing needed; the function of the state should begin and end with insistence on some kind of education, and, if possible, a kind which promotes mental individualism, not a kind which happens to conform to the prejudices of government officials.

III

Questions of practical morals raise more difficult problems than questions of mere opinion. The thugs honestly believe it their duty to commit murders, but the government does not acquiesce. The conscientious objectors honestly hold the opposite opinion, and again the government does not acquiesce. Killing is a state prerogative; it is equally criminal to do it unbidden and not to do it when bidden. The same applies to theft, unless it is on a large scale or by one who is already rich. Thugs and thieves are men who use force in their dealings with their neighbors, and we may lay it down broadly that the private use of force should be prohibited except in rare cases, however conscientious may be its motive. But this principle will not justify compelling men to use force at the bidding of the state, when they do not believe it justified by the occasion. The punishment of conscientious objectors seems clearly a violation of individual liberty within its legitimate sphere.

It is generally assumed without question that the state has a right to punish certain kinds of sexual irregularity. No one doubts that the Mormons sincerely believed polygamy to be a desirable practice, yet the United States required them to abandon its legal recognition, and probably any other Christian country would have done likewise. Nevertheless, I do not think this prohibition was wise. Polygamy is legally permitted in many parts of the world, but is not much practised except by chiefs and potentates. If, as Europeans generally believe, it is an undesirable custom, it is probable that the Mormons would have soon abandoned it, except perhaps for a few men of exceptional position. If, on the other hand, it had proved a successful experiment, the world would have acquired a piece of knowledge which it is now unable to possess. I think in all such cases the law should only intervene when there is some injury inflicted without the consent of the injured person.

It is obvious that men and women would not tolerate having their wives or husbands selected by the state, whatever eugenists might have to say in favor of such a plan. In this it seems clear that ordinary public opinion is in the right, not because people choose wisely, but because any choice of their own is better than a forced marriage. What applies to marriage ought also to apply to the choice of a trade or profession; although some men have no marked preferences, most men greatly prefer some occupations to others, and are far more likely to be useful citizens if they follow their preferences than if they are thwarted by a public authority.

The case of the man who has an intense conviction that he ought to do a certain kind of work is peculiar, and perhaps not very common; but it is important because it includes some very important individuals. Joan of Arc and Florence Nightingale defied convention in obedience to a feeling of this sort; reformers and agitators in unpopular causes, such as Mazzini, have belonged to this class; so have many men of science. In cases of this kind the individual conviction deserves the greatest respect, even if there seems no obvious justification for it. Obedience to the impulse is very unlikely to do much harm, and may well do great good. The practical difficulty is to distinguish such impulses from desires which produce similar manifestations. Many young people wish to be authors without having an impulse to write any particular book, or wish to be painters without having an impulse to create any particular picture. But a little experience will usually show the difference between a genuine and a spurious impulse; and there is less harm in indulging the spurious impulse for a time than in thwarting the impulse which is genuine. Nevertheless, the plain man almost always has a tendency to thwart the genuine impulse, because it seems anarchic and unreasonable, and is seldom able to give a good account of itself in advance.

What is markedly true of some notable personalities is true, in a lesser degree, of almost every individual who has much vigor or force of life; there is an impulse towards activity of some kind, as a rule not very definite in youth, but growing gradually more sharply outlined under the influence of education and opportunity. The direct impulse toward a kind of activity for its own sake must be distinguished from the desire for the expected effects of the activity. A young man may desire the rewards of great achievement without having any spontaneous impulse toward the activities which lead to achievement. But those who actually achieve much, although they may desire the rewards, have also something in their nature which inclines them to choose a certain kind of work as the road which they must travel if their ambition is to be satisfied. This artist's impulse, as it may be called, is a thing of infinite value to the individual, and often to the world; to respect it in oneself and in others makes up nine tenths of the good life. In most human beings it is rather frail, rather easily destroyed or disturbed; parents and teachers are too often hostile to it, and our economic system crushes out its last remnants in young men and young women. The result is that human beings cease to be individual, or to retain the native pride that is their birthright; they become machine-made, tame, convenient for the bureaucrat and the drill-sergeant, capable of being tabulated in statistics without anything being omitted. This is the fundamental evil resulting from lack of liberty; and it is an evil which is being continually intensified as population grows more dense and the machinery of organization grows more efficient.

The things that men desire are many and various: admiration, affection, power, security, ease, outlets for energy, are among the commonest of motives. But such abstractions do not touch what makes the difference between one man and another. Whenever I go to the zoölogical gardens, I am struck by the fact that all the movements of a stork have some common quality, differing from the movements of a parrot or an ostrich. It is impossible to put in words what the common quality is, and yet we feel that each thing an animal does is the sort of thing we might expect that animal to do. This indefinable quality constitutes the individuality of the animal, and gives rise to the pleasure we feel in watching the animal's actions. In a human being, provided he has not been crushed by an economic or governmental machine, there is the same kind of individuality, a something distinctive without which no man or woman can achieve much of importance, or retain the full dignity which is native to human beings. It is this distinctive individuality that is loved by the artist, whether painter or writer. The artist himself, and the man who is creative in no matter what direction, has more of it than the average man. Any society which crushes this quality, whether intentionally or by accident, must soon become utterly lifeless and traditional, without hope of progress and without any purpose in its being. To preserve and strengthen the impulse that makes individuality should be the foremost object of all political institutions.

IV

We now arrive at certain general principles in regard to individual liberty and public control.

The greater part of human impulses may be divided into two classes, those which are possessive and those which are constructive or creative. Social institutions are the garments or embodiments of impulses, and may be classified roughly according to the impulses which they embody. Property is the direct expression of possessiveness; science and art are among the most direct expressions of creativeness. Possessiveness is either defensive or aggressive; it seeks either to retain against a robber, or to acquire from a present holder. In either case an attitude of hostility toward others is of its essence. It would be a mistake to suppose that defensive possessiveness is always justifiable, while the aggressive kind is always blameworthy; where there is great injustice in the *status quo*, the exact opposite may be the case, and ordinarily neither is justifiable.

State interference with the actions of individuals is necessitated by possessiveness. Some goods can be acquired or retained by force, while others cannot. A wife can be acquired by force, as the Romans acquired the Sabine women; but a wife's affection cannot be acquired in this way. There is no record that the Romans desired the affection of the Sabine women; and those in whom possessive impulses are strong tend to care chiefly for the goods that force can secure. All material goods belong to this class. Liberty in regard to such goods, if it were unrestricted, would make the strong rich and the weak poor. In a capitalistic society, owing to the partial restraints imposed by law, it makes cunning men rich and honest men poor, because the force of the state is put at men's disposal, not according to any just or rational principle, but according to a set of traditional maxims of which the explanation is purely historical.

In all that concerns possession and the use of force, unrestrained liberty involves anarchy and injustice. Freedom to kill, freedom to rob, freedom to defraud, no longer belong to individuals, though they still belong to great states, and are exercised by them in the name of patriotism. Neither individuals nor states ought to be free to exert force on their own initiative, except in such sudden emergencies as will subsequently be admitted in justification by a court of law. The reason for this is that the exertion of force by one individual against another is always an evil on both sides, and can only be tolerated when it is compensated by some overwhelming resultant good. In order to minimize the amount of force actually exerted in the world, it is necessary that there should be a public authority, a repository of practically irresistible force, whose function should be primarily to repress the private use of force. A use of force is *private* when it is exerted by one of the interested parties, or by his friends or accomplices, not by a public neutral authority according to some rule which is intended to be in the public interest.

The régime of private property under which we live does much too little to restrain the private use of force. When a man owns a piece of land, for example, he may use force against trespassers, though they must not use force against him. It is clear that some restriction of the liberty of trespass is necessary for the cultivation of the land. But if such powers are to be given to an individual, the state ought to satisfy itself that he occupies no more land than he is warranted in occupying in the public interest, and that the share of the produce of the land that comes to him is no more than a just reward for his labors. Probably the only way in which such ends can be achieved is by state ownership of land. The possessors of land and capital are able at present, by economic pressure, to use force against those who have no possessions. This force is sanctioned by law, while force exercised by the poor against the rich is illegal. Such a state of things is unjust, and does not diminish the use of private force as much as it might be diminished.

The whole realm of the possessive impulses, and of the use of force to which they give rise, stands in need of control by a public neutral authority, in the interests of liberty no less than of justice. Within a nation, this public authority will naturally be the state; in relations between nations, if the present anarchy is to cease, it will have to be some international parliament.

But the motive underlying the public control of men's possessive impulses should always be the increase of liberty, both by the prevention of private tyranny and by the liberation of creative impulses. If public control is not to do more harm than good, it must be so exercised as to leave the utmost freedom of private initiative in all those ways that do not involve the private use of force. In this respect all governments have always failed egregiously, and there is no evidence that they are improving.

The creative impulses, unlike those that are possessive, are directed to ends in which one man's gain is not another man's loss. The man who makes a scientific discovery or writes a poem is enriching others at the same time as himself. Any increase in knowledge or good-will is a gain to all who are affected by it, not only to the actual possessor. Those who feel the joy of life are a happiness to others as well as to themselves. Force cannot create such things, though it can destroy them; no principle of distributive justice applies to them, since the gain of each is the gain of all. For these reasons, the creative part of a man's activity ought to be as free as possible from all public control, in order that it may remain spontaneous and full of vigor. The only function of the state in regard to this part of the individual life should be to do everything possible toward providing outlets and opportunities.

In every life a part is governed by the community, and a part by private initiative. The part governed by private initiative is greatest in the most important individuals, such as men of genius and creative thinkers. This part ought only to be restricted when it is predatory; otherwise, everything ought to be done to make it as great and as vigorous as possible. The object of education ought not to be to make all men think alike, but to make each think in the way which is the fullest expression of his own personality. In the choice of a means of livelihood all young men and young women ought, as far as possible, to be able to choose what is attractive to them; if no money-making occupation is attractive, they ought to be free to do little work for little pay, and spend their leisure as they choose. Any kind of censure on freedom of thought or on the dissemination of knowledge is, of course, to be condemned utterly.

Huge organizations, both political and economic, are one of the distinguishing characteristics of the modern world. These organizations have immense power, and often use their power to discourage originality in thought and action. They ought, on the contrary, to give the freest scope that is possible without producing anarchy or violent conflict. They ought not to take cognizance of any part of a man's life except what is concerned with the legitimate objects of public control, namely, possessions and the use of force. And they ought, by devolution, to leave as large a share of control as possible in the hands of individuals and small groups. If this is not done, the men at the head of these vast organizations will infallibly become tyrannous through the habit of excessive power, and will in time interfere in ways that crush out individual initiative.

The problem which faces the modern world is the combination of individual initiative with the increase in the scope and size of organizations. Unless it is solved, individuals will grow less and less full of life and vigor, and more and more passively submissive to conditions imposed upon them. A society composed of such individuals cannot be progressive or add much to the world's stock of mental and spiritual possessions. Only personal liberty and the encouragement of initiative can secure these things. Those who resist authority when it encroaches upon the legitimate sphere of the individual are performing a service to society, however little society may value it. In regard to the past, this is universally acknowledged; but it is no less true in regard to the present and the future.

CHAPTER V

National Independence and Internationalism

In the relations between states, as in the relations of groups within a single state, what is to be desired is independence for each as regards internal affairs, and law rather than private force as regards external affairs. But as regards groups within a state, it is internal independence that must be emphasized, since that is what is lacking; subjection to law has been secured, on the whole, since the end of the Middle Ages. In the relations between states, on the contrary, it is law and a central government that are lacking, since independence exists for external as for internal affairs. The stage we have reached in the affairs of Europe corresponds to the stage reached in our internal affairs during the Wars of the Roses, when turbulent barons frustrated the attempt to make them keep the king's peace. Thus, although the goal is the same in the two cases, the steps to be taken in order to achieve it are quite different.

There can be no good international system until the boundaries of states coincide as nearly as possible with the boundaries of nations.

But it is not easy to say what we mean by a nation. Are the Irish a nation? Home Rulers say yes, Unionists say no. Are the Ulstermen a nation? Unionists say yes, Home Rulers say no. In all such cases it is a party question whether we are to call a group a nation or not. A German will tell you that the Russian Poles are a nation, but as for the Prussian Poles, they, of course, are part of Prussia. Professors can always be hired to prove, by arguments of race or language or history, that a group about which there is a dispute is, or is not, a nation, as may be desired by those whom the professors serve. If we are to avoid all these controversies, we must first of all endeavor to find some definition of a nation.

A nation is not to be defined by affinities of language or a common historical origin, though these things often help to produce a nation. Switzerland is a nation, despite diversities of race, religion, and language. England and Scotland now form one nation, though they did not do so at the time of the Civil War. This is shown by Cromwell's saying, in the height of the conflict, that he would rather be subject to the domain of the royalists than to that of the Scotch. Great Britain was one state before it was one nation; on the other hand, Germany was one nation before it was one state.

What constitutes a nation is a sentiment and an instinct, a sentiment of similarity and an instinct of belonging to the same group or herd. The instinct is an extension of the instinct which constitutes a flock of sheep, or any other group of gregarious animals. The sentiment which goes with this is like a milder and more extended form of family feeling. When we return to England after being on the Continent, we feel something friendly in the familiar ways, and it is easy to believe that Englishmen on the whole are virtuous, while many foreigners are full of designing wickedness.

Such feelings make it easy to organize a nation into a state. It is not difficult, as a rule, to acquiesce in the orders of a national government. We feel that it is our government, and that its decrees are more or less the same as those which we should have given if we ourselves had been the governors. There is an instinctive and usually unconscious sense of a common purpose animating the members of a nation. This becomes especially vivid when there is war or a danger of war. Any one who, at such a time, stands out against the orders of his government feels an inner conflict quite different from any that he would feel in standing out against the orders of a foreign government in whose power he might happen to find himself. If he stands out, he does so with some more or less conscious hope that his government may in time come to think as he does; whereas, in standing out against a foreign government, no such hope is necessary. This group instinct, however it may have arisen, is what constitutes a nation, and what makes it important that the boundaries of nations should also be the boundaries of states.

National sentiment is a fact, and should be taken account of by institutions. When it is ignored, it is intensified and becomes a source of strife. It can only be rendered harmless by being given free play, so long as it is not predatory. But it is not, in itself, a good or admirable feeling. There is nothing rational and nothing desirable in a limitation of sympathy which confines it to a fragment of the human race. Diversities of manners and customs and traditions are, on the whole, a good thing, since they enable different nations to produce different types of excellence. But in national feeling there is always latent or explicit an element of hostility to foreigners. National feeling, as we know it, could not exist in a nation which was wholly free from external pressure of a hostile kind.

And group feeling produces a limited and often harmful kind of morality. Men come to identify the good with what serves the interests of their own group, and the bad with what works against those interests, even if it should happen to be in the interests of mankind as a whole. This group morality is very much in evidence during war, and is taken for granted in men's ordinary thought. Although almost all Englishmen consider the defeat of Germany desirable for the good of the world, yet nevertheless most of them honor a German for fighting for his country, because it has not occurred to them that his actions ought to be guided by a morality higher than that of the group.

A man does right, as a rule, to have his thoughts more occupied with the interests of his own nation than with those of others, because his actions are more likely to affect his own nation. But in time of war, and in all matters which are of equal concern to other nations and to his own, a man ought to take account of the universal welfare, and not allow his survey to be limited by the interest, or supposed interest, of his own group or nation.

So long as national feeling exists, it is very important that each nation should be self-governing as regards its internal affairs. Government can only be carried on by force and tyranny if its subjects view it with hostile eyes, and they will so view it if they feel that it belongs to an alien nation. This principle meets with difficulties in cases where men of different nations live side by side in the same area, as happens in some parts of the Balkans. There are also difficulties in regard to places which, for some geographical reason, are of great international importance, such as the Suez Canal and the Panama Canal. In such cases the purely local desires of the inhabitants may have to give way before larger interests. But in general, at any rate as applied to civilized communities, the principle that the boundaries of nations ought to coincide with the boundaries of states has very few exceptions.

This principle, however, does not decide how the relations between states are to be regulated, or how a conflict of interests between rival states is to be decided. At present, every great state claims absolute sovereignty, not only in regard to its internal affairs but also in regard to its external actions. This claim to absolute sovereignty leads it into conflict with similar claims on the part of other great states. Such conflicts at present can only be decided by war or diplomacy, and diplomacy is in essence nothing but the threat of war. There is no more justification for the claim to absolute sovereignty on the part of a state than there would be for a similar claim on the part of an individual. The claim to absolute sovereignty is, in effect, a claim that all external affairs are to be regulated purely by force, and that when two nations or groups of nations are interested in a question, the decision shall depend solely upon which of them is, or is believed to be, the stronger. This is nothing but primitive anarchy, "the war of all against all," which Hobbes asserted to be the original state of mankind.

There cannot be secure peace in the world, or any decision of international questions according to international law, until states are willing to part with their absolute sovereignty as regards their external relations, and to leave the decision in such matters to some international instrument of government.[5] An international government will have to be legislative as well as judicial. It is not enough that there should be a Hague tribunal, deciding matters according to some already existing system of international law; it is necessary also that there should be a body capable of enacting international law, and this body will have to have the power of transferring territory from one state to another, when it is persuaded that adequate grounds exist for such a transference. Friends of peace will make a mistake if they unduly glorify the *status quo*. Some nations grow, while others dwindle; the population of an area may change its character by emigration and immigration. There is no good reason why states should resent changes in their boundaries under such

[5] For detailed scheme of international government see "International Government," by L. Woolf. Allen & Unwin.

conditions, and if no international authority has power to make changes of this kind, the temptations to war will sometimes become irresistible.

The international authority ought to possess an army and navy, and these ought to be the only army and navy in existence. The only legitimate use of force is to diminish the total amount of force exercised in the world. So long as men are free to indulge their predatory instincts, some men or groups of men will take advantage of this freedom for oppression and robbery. Just as the police are necessary to prevent the use of force by private citizens, so an international police will be necessary to prevent the lawless use of force by separate states.

But I think it is reasonable to hope that if ever an international government, possessed of the only army and navy in the world, came into existence, the need of force to enact obedience to its decisions would be very temporary. In a short time the benefits resulting from the substitution of law for anarchy would become so obvious that the international government would acquire an unquestioned authority, and no state would dream of rebelling against its decisions. As soon as this stage had been reached, the international army and navy would become unnecessary.

We have still a very long road to travel before we arrive at the establishment of an international authority, but it is not very difficult to foresee the steps by which this result will be gradually reached. There is likely to be a continual increase in the practice of submitting disputes to arbitration, and in the realization that the supposed conflicts of interest between different states are mainly illusory. Even where there is a real conflict of interest, it must in time become obvious that neither of the states concerned would suffer as much by giving way as by fighting. With the progress of inventions, war, when it does occur, is bound to become increasingly destructive. The civilized races of the world are faced with the alternative of coöperation or mutual destruction. The present war is making this alternative daily more evident. And it is difficult to believe that, when the enmities which it has generated have had time to cool, civilized men will deliberately choose to destroy civilization, rather than acquiesce in the abolition of war.

The matters in which the interests of nations are supposed to clash are mainly three: tariffs, which are a delusion; the exploitation of inferior races, which is a crime; pride of power and dominion, which is a schoolboy folly.

The economic argument against tariffs is familiar, and I shall not repeat it. The only reason why it fails to carry conviction is the enmity between nations. Nobody proposes to set up a tariff between England and Scotland, or between Lancashire and Yorkshire. Yet the arguments by which tariffs between nations are supported might be used just as well to defend tariffs between counties. Universal free trade would indubitably be of economic benefit to mankind, and would be adopted to-morrow if it were not for the hatred and suspicion which nations feel one toward another. From the point of view of preserving the peace of the world, free trade between the different civilized states is not so important as the open door in their dependencies. The desire for exclusive markets is one of the most potent causes of war.

Exploiting what are called "inferior races" has become one of the main objects of European statecraft. It is not only, or primarily, trade that is desired, but opportunities for investment; finance is more concerned in the matter than industry. Rival diplomatists are very often the servants, conscious or unconscious, of rival groups of financiers. The financiers, though themselves of no particular nation, understand the art of appealing to national prejudice, and of inducing the taxpayer to incur expenditure of which they reap the benefit. The evils which they produce at home, and the devastation that they spread among the races whom they exploit, are part of the price which the world has to pay for its acquiescence in the capitalist régime.

But neither tariffs nor financiers would be able to cause serious trouble, if it were not for the sentiment of national pride. National pride might be on the whole beneficent, if it took the direction of emulation in the things that are important to civilization. If we prided ourselves upon our poets, our men of science, or the justice and humanity of our social system, we might find in national pride a stimulus to useful endeavors. But such matters play a very small part. National pride, as it exists now, is almost exclusively concerned with power and dominion, with the extent of territory that a nation owns, and with its capacity for enforcing its will against the opposition of other nations. In this it is reinforced by group morality. To nine citizens out of ten it seems self-evident, whenever the will of their own nation clashes with that of another, that their own nation must be in the right. Even if it were not in the right on the particular issue, yet it stands in general for so much nobler ideals than those represented by the other nation to the dispute, that any increase in its power is bound to be for the good of mankind. Since all nations equally believe this of themselves, all are equally ready to insist upon the victory of their own side in any dispute in which they believe that they have a good hope of victory. While this temper persists, the hope of international coöperation must remain dim.

If men could divest themselves of the sentiment of rivalry and hostility between different nations, they would perceive that the matters in which the interests of different nations coincide immeasurably outweigh those in which they clash; they would perceive, to begin with, that trade is not to be compared to warfare; that the man who sells you goods is not doing you an injury. No one considers that the butcher and the baker are his enemies because they drain him of money. Yet as soon as goods come from a foreign country, we are asked to believe that we suffer a terrible injury in purchasing them. No one remembers that it is by means of goods exported that we purchase them. But in the country to which we export, it is the goods we send which are thought dangerous, and the goods we buy are forgotten. The whole conception of trade, which has been forced upon us by manufacturers who dreaded foreign competition, by trusts which desired to secure monopolies, and by economists poisoned by the virus of nationalism, is totally and absolutely false. Trade results simply from division of labor. A man cannot himself make all the goods of which he has need, and therefore he must exchange his produce with that of other people. What applies to the individual, applies in exactly the same way to the nation. There is no reason to desire that a nation should itself produce all the goods of which it has need; it is better that it should specialize upon those goods which it can produce to most advantage, and should exchange its surplus with the surplus of other goods produced by other countries. There is no use in sending goods out of the country except in order to get other goods in return. A butcher who is always willing to part with his meat but not willing to take bread from the baker, or boots from the bootmaker, or clothes from the tailor, would soon find himself in a sorry plight. Yet he would be no more foolish than the protectionist who desires that we should send goods abroad without receiving payment in the shape of goods imported from abroad.

The wage system has made people believe that what a man needs is work. This, of course, is absurd. What he needs is the goods produced by work, and the less work involved in making a given amount of goods, the better. But owing to our economic system, every economy in methods of production enables employers to dismiss some of their employees, and to cause destitution, where a better system would produce only an increase of wages or a diminution in the hours of work without any corresponding diminution of wages.

Our economic system is topsyturvy. It makes the interest of the individual conflict with the interest of the community in a thousand ways in which no such conflict ought to exist. Under a better system the benefits of free trade and the evils of tariffs would be obvious to all.

Apart from trade, the interests of nations coincide in all that makes what we call civilization. Inventions and discoveries bring benefit to all. The progress of science is a matter of equal concern to the whole civilized world. Whether a man of science is an Englishman, a Frenchman, or a German is a matter of no real importance. His discoveries are open to all, and nothing but intelligence is required in order to profit by them. The whole world of art and literature and learning is international; what is done in one country is not done for that country, but for mankind. If we ask ourselves what are the things that raise mankind above the brutes, what are the things that make us think the human race more valuable than any species of animals, we shall find that none of them are things in which any one nation can have exclusive property, but all are things in which the whole world can share. Those who have any care for these things, those who wish to see mankind fruitful in the work which men alone can do, will take little account of national boundaries, and have little care to what state a man happens to owe allegiance.

The importance of international coöperation outside the sphere of politics has been brought home to me by my own experience. Until lately I was engaged in teaching a new science which few men in the world were able to teach. My own work in this science was based chiefly upon the work of a German and an Italian. My pupils came from all over the civilized world:

France, Germany, Austria, Russia, Greece, Japan, China, India, and America. None of us was conscious of any sense of national divisions. We felt ourselves an outpost of civilization, building a new road into the virgin forest of the unknown. All coöperated in the common task, and in the interest of such a work the political enmities of nations seemed trivial, temporary, and futile.

But it is not only in the somewhat rarefied atmosphere of abstruse science that international coöperation is vital to the progress of civilization. All our economic problems, all the questions of securing the rights of labor, all the hopes of freedom at home and humanity abroad, rest upon the creation of international good-will.

So long as hatred, suspicion, and fear dominate the feelings of men toward each other, so long we cannot hope to escape from the tyranny of violence and brute force. Men must learn to be conscious of the common interests of mankind in which all are at one, rather than of those supposed interests in which the nations are divided. It is not necessary, or even desirable, to obliterate the differences of manners and custom and tradition between different nations. These differences enable each nation to make its own distinctive contribution to the sum total of the world's civilization.

What is to be desired is not cosmopolitanism, not the absence of all national characteristics that one associates with couriers, *wagon-lit* attendants, and others, who have had everything distinctive obliterated by multiple and trivial contacts with men of every civilized country. Such cosmopolitanism is the result of loss, not gain. The international spirit which we should wish to see produced will be something added to love of country, not something taken away. Just as patriotism does not prevent a man from feeling family affection, so the international spirit ought not to prevent a man from feeling affection for his own country.

But it will somewhat alter the character of that affection. The things which he will desire for his own country will no longer be things which can only be acquired at the expense of others, but rather those things in which the excellence of any one country is to the advantage of all the world. He will wish his own country to be great in the arts of peace, to be eminent in thought and science, to be magnanimous and just and generous. He will wish it to help mankind on the way toward that better world of liberty and international concord which must be realized if any happiness is to be left to man. He will not desire for his country the passing triumphs of a narrow possessiveness, but rather the enduring triumph of having helped to embody in human affairs something of that spirit of brotherhood which Christ taught and which the Christian churches have forgotten. He will see that this spirit embodies not only the highest morality, but also the truest wisdom, and the only road by which the nations, torn and bleeding with the wounds which scientific madness has inflicted, can emerge into a life where growth is possible and joy is not banished at the frenzied call of unreal and fictitious duties. Deeds inspired by hate are not duties, whatever pain and self-sacrifice they may involve. Life and hope for the world are to be found only in the deeds of love.

www.ingramcontent.com/pod-product-compliance
Lightning Source LLC
Chambersburg PA
CBHW022202160726
48282CB00024B/293
* 9 7 8 9 3 5 5 2 2 3 0 8 1 *